The Sandpaper Effect

10 ways to spark the entrepreneur in kids!

ISBN 978-0-615-35292-3

Contents

Foreword

To customize our lives … that is the answer!

Being happy, feeling secure, enjoying and exercising one's freedom, whether creative, intellectual, spiritual, or financial. These are the basic desires of people the world over, the very essence of what separates rational, purposeful man from conditioned, unreflective beast. So how is it that so few among us can lay claim to having attained these basic human desires, or at least doing so in a continual meaningful way? Why are the truly liberated the exception rather than the norm?

While these questions certainly are not limited to any single answer, it is difficult to discount the influence of practicality, of conditioning, of real life. We love our houses, but they usually come paired with a pesky detail called a mortgage. We cherish our children, but for the better part of twenty years the financial, emotional, and logistical burden they impose can be nothing short of crippling. Adding to the frustration of feeling constrained by life's demands is knowing that somewhere below the surface of an increasingly static, other-driven existence still burns that innate and uniquely human desire to be self-directed, self-sufficient, self-fulfilled.

How, then, to reverse course and throw off the chains – sometimes self-affixed – of what keeps us from being who and what we naturally are? Recognizing how difficult it is to become un-conditioned to the ways of modern life, we might look instead to the pre-conditioned – those in whom the inner drive to be creative and self-propelled has not yet been dampened – and endeavor to spark, foster, and cultivate in them the entrepreneurial spirit that lay dormant in most of us.

In *"The Sandpaper Effect,"* Jamar Milsap, through an inventive and entertaining mix of personal anecdote and honest introspection, offers a roadmap for how parents can equip their children with the tools necessary to set their natural

entrepreneurial drive in motion. The title itself —
based on Milsap's own account as a child talking with
and learning from his resourceful, enterprising father
— provides the perfect backdrop to Milsap's personal
journey from curious, creative adolescent to
independent-minded, self-made adult.

How fitting, then, that just when Milsap takes the
next step in his entrepreneurial journey — from
student, to doer, and now to motivator — America
seems to need it the most. If the past few years have
taught us anything, it's that those who are best able
to determine their own fate, rather than be at the
mercy of large corporations and volatile economies,
are the most likely to be unaffected when downturns
occur. The message is simple: equip our children with
the skills they'll need to be their own boss, to write
their own ticket to happiness and fulfillment. They
already have the desire; all they need is the guidance.
Milsap, in laying out a comprehensive framework, has
done his part. Will you do yours?

Tony Dejarnette

Money is an idea ...

"How much for a cup of lemonade?" the customer asked.

"That will be 50 cents," we answered.

"Ok, I'll take a cup," the customer said.

As we prepared the customer's drink, he passed us a dollar bill and said, "Keep the change, I'm proud to see young men out here doing positive things, making money the right way." Thus began the L-block entrepreneur mind set. Led by ideas from the adventurous and daring mind of Sap (Jamar Milsap), we were able to creatively develop various ways of earning money. From cutting grass to selling Avon beauty supplies, each endeavor provided us with valuable life lessons.

The world is changing. Rarely do you find a worker remaining with one employer for 30 years. To receive your true value in today's work place, you now have to move from company to company for a well deserved promotion, even then not receiving a fair raise. By being an entrepreneur, you earn the fruit of your hard work. You have a better chance of controlling your fate. Tools learned in this book will better prepare your child, nephew or even yourself to be future entrepreneurs.

Take a good look at today's economic climate. Corporate jobs used to be considered safe, and therefore attracted more individuals who were willing to trade 30 years or more of their productive life to one company, for a chance to be part of helping to build that company and providing the company with valuable ideas – your ideas. This places a "financial cap" on us. Increasingly companies are engaging in more workforce reduction tactics in an effort to meet their financial targets. Why not control your own fate without limiting yourself financially. Read this book, follow the exercises, and use the tools given. As a parent, I know that we are tasked with helping to ensure the future of our children – providing them with a better opportunity. Giving a child the tools to succeed, preparing them for the future, that's what this book is about. Tomorrow is today, will your child be ready?

Todd Allen

Acknowledgements

We all experience times of clarity with each milestone of our lives. For the past few years I've continued to seek something fulfilling that involved working with children. My parents were very influential in setting the proper example. As a child I was frequently scolded to the proper degree. Each conversation with my dad ended with him saying to me, "I'm trying to teach you how to be a man."

My childhood was full of adventures. There were six of us in the home including my parents. My siblings and I were close in age as we were only separated by two to three years. As I wrote this book I couldn't help but think of each of them and the contribution they made to my life, setting the foundation of this book.

First, I'd like to thank my big sister Lisa, who always made sure we followed mom and dad's house rules. I remember clearly the days of not being able to open Christmas presents until 7 a.m. Lisa held her ground and was able to hold me back from breaking that rule. She taught me discipline and after memorizing the entire Michael Jackson thriller video under her lead I knew I could take on just about anything.

Then there is my big brother Juan. Similar to my big sister, Juan's demeanor was always cool and calm. He never got too angry or upset which helped set the tone for me. He always looked out for my personal development, which included continual encouragement and the occasional gifts of "big brother" money when I needed it.

My younger sister, Tamika, and I were similar. She was bold and verbal, and never backed down from a challenge. Just as a superhero has a grand nemesis, she was mine. No matter the size of our home growing up, it wasn't big enough for both our egos and attitudes. As time went on, I came to appreciate the fact that I had to work hard to earn the "big brother" title and in my eyes she will always be my little sister.

Many words can be used to describe my mom Carol. She kept order in the house and she wielded her power well. I attempted to challenge her continuously but she always made it clear who the boss was. As a grown man I still get chills when she gives me "the look." She always taught me to be respectable and when others tell me I'm a good person all the thanks and gratitude should really go to her.

Last but not least, is my father Tex. He was what one could easily call the Jack of all Trades. A typical day would consist of him rising at 5 a.m. and leaving the house by 6 a.m. to nurture the plants in his garden. Then he would set off to the first of many odd jobs for the day. Sometimes, after work, he stopped at one of his local hangouts for a game of billiards along with a few magic tricks for fun. The day would end with another trip to his garden picking up vegetables to bring home or give away. Once home, he would have his dinner, enjoy a few laughs with the family and watch his favorite nature television programs to conclude the night.

I've taken many things from my father but the most important would be the lesson in being well-rounded. He taught me to have no enemies, but instead to be diplomatic; ensuring that everyone would have a fair chance.

Family bonds are stronger than any other tie. The early influences are so critical to our future development. I had many aunts, uncles and cousins who've always supported me in everything. My Uncle Dennis and Aunt Carolyn were key in making sure I stayed on the right track and my grandfather made sure I took time to relax and enjoy life. My Uncle Kevin and Aunt Darlene both proved to be role models as I matured and many summers were spent with my cousins Dennis, Dennean, Danisha, Brittany and Brandice.

There remains one last group of people to name, those who were the center of my childhood experiences, my close friends: Todd, Tony, Billy, Chuck, LeRoy, Rick, Mike, JC, Keith, Carl, Clifford, Kendrick, Damon, Daria, Yvette, Antoinette, Stacy and Sheree. What we encountered as kids set the tone for our own children and it was something I'll never forget. It wouldn't be fair to leave out the parents who were there to help keep us in order. In that regard, I acknowledge Cheryl Allen-Spells, Colleen Hill, Ruth Friend, Ms. Beverly, Ms. Kay, Mr. & Mrs. Nickerson, Adrienne Selby, Mr. & Mrs. Riley, Mr. & Mrs. Stillis, Gretchen and Mr. & Mrs. Carroll. I would also like to thank Jehovah for opening my eyes to the truth. Without it I would be in complete darkness.

Last but not least, I would like to send a resounding thank you to Davinah for her undying love, patience and support.

Introduction

Everything that has a beginning has an end! That phrase was taken from my favorite movie trilogy of all time, "The Matrix." We experience all kinds of things as a child. We go through the phase of wants surpassing needs and then simply wanting anything that has some sort of appeal. It's our parents' jobs to help reel us back into reality, understanding that we simply can't have whatever we want, or can we?

The Sandpaper Effect is a book that examines the possible transformation from child to entrepreneur. Children are born with the innate ability to explore before the abilities to talk and walk develop. It's simply embedded in their DNA. In this new millennium it's not uncommon to see an increasing number of young people begin to build and run successful companies even before they graduate from college. For some of us, our parents lived during a time where hard work and longevity at companies was the accepted norm. We no longer have deep 401(k)s or retirement plans that will allow us to sip Mai Tai's in Tahiti for the rest of our lives. It's now the DIY (do-it-yourself) era where millionaires are made overnight, where you can custom design your life if you apply yourself and keep moving forward. This book is designed to ignite a spark, and inspire, kids and parents worldwide to be perpetual explorers.

This will also be a journey of my experiences as a kid and how the things my mother and father taught me helped spark the ambition and drive needed to succeed. Time and circumstance can sometimes instantly alter one's course in life. Some of these circumstances can be pleasant, fun, even exciting, while others can be dark, dreary and outright sad. It all comes down to how we play the game of life. Similar to Monopoly, we try to cover enough ground to collect $200 whenever we pass go. I hope this book will inspire you to challenge and spark that drive in your child. If you don't have kids, the same can be done with nephews or nieces or it can help you if you're thinking of becoming a parent.

1

FEEL MY HANDS

My father was born and raised in a small town in Mississippi. He relocated to Philadelphia as a teenager. As long as I've known my dad, his determination and perseverance far surpassed that of any superhero or fictitious character one could imagine. I say this for many reasons. First, my dad always created something from nothing and second, he never accepted defeat when it came to a challenge, even though over the years he has failed at many things just like everyone else. My father's family didn't have much when he was growing up and due to the strong financial needs to maintain the household he was pulled out of school in the second grade. This wasn't that unusual given that he was raised in the Great Depression, but nonetheless it caused him a tremendous amount of stress.

As a result of his limited education my father did all that he could to make ends meet. This would be the early beginnings of his hustling days. A hustler is defined as an enterprising person determined to succeed, hence a go-getter, and these were skills my father acquired as a means of survival. There were six of us in the house and we didn't have a ton of things, but we got by. I remember going downstairs in the morning before school to find a couple one dollar bills that one of my parents had placed on the coffee table for me to buy lunch. Each night, my mom prepared what we thought were the best meals for our family dinners, which we would eat when my dad arrived home. The dinner table was also the first place where I received my initial commercial lesson.

My dad worked for a large construction company and he was very skilled in his field, so much so that he would generate extra income on the weekends by doing odd jobs around the neighborhood. He quickly became the "go-to" guy whenever anyone needed a sidewalk to be built, an addition to their deck made or any other general construction. There were no business cards or fancy advertisements, just my dad going around and asking neighbors if they needed anything done. Each evening my father would come in the house, head straight to the shower, immediately after which he would lie flat on his back on the living room floor. I always wondered why my father was so exhausted so I would repeatedly ask him. After explaining a few times, he decided to give me my first lesson.

He called me close to him and said, "Feel my hands." Initially I didn't understand what he was doing, but little did I know this lesson would stick with me the rest of my life. Working in the construction field required continual use of his hands and in spite of wearing construction gloves throughout the day his hands were still very worn. When my young child's hands touched my father's rugged, work-worn hands my facial expression changed as if I'd just eaten Brussels sprouts or something equally unpleasant.

My father's hands were so coarse and rough that I told him they felt like sandpaper. He revealed a sly grin and said, "You're right and here's what I want you to learn." He said, "No matter what happens in life always think first and study; read, learn, observe and be open to whatever comes your way." Of course I would ask what that had to do with his hands feeling like shattered glass and he would say, "I didn't learn as much nor did I have an education so I have to do hard work. If you continue to do good in school, as you are, and apply yourself your hands will never feel this way, regardless of what position you may end up having in life."

From that day forward he would do this exercise at least three times a week, almost to the point where I became very upset and that was rule #1 – ***The Power of Choice!***

To expound on this point, my dad was simply teaching me that there are many ways to make money. Some are much tougher than others but the more I used my brain and applied myself, the less difficult things would become when it came to work.

Of course, as a child, the only things I cared about were Nintendo and eating peanut butter and jelly sandwiches, so it took some time for this notion to become solidified. It really stuck when I saw the latest advertisement for Air Jordan sneakers or a new video game being released.

I was always amazed at how quickly my father could generate income. For example, I would go in and tell him on a Monday that I needed shoes because mine were worn and he would simply nod his head and tell me he'd work on it. By this time, I was aware of his payment schedule (every 2 weeks on a Friday) so I assumed it would be a few days, but the very next day he came home with the money I needed for new shoes. I was tempted to ask how he got it so fast, but my mother gave me a stern look so I decided against it.

These early lessons from my father instilled a sense of risk taking in me. At present, we live in a time where it appears that employees have become nothing more than faceless numbers and when stock prices and values plummet, so does everyone's morale. There are numerous stories and examples of people who either completely lose faith when they lose a job, or were unsuccessful in receiving that bonus or training needed to get that raise. As children, we're taught that failure is bad and winning is everything, but what is left out is the fact that failure is sometimes necessary in order to win. The sandpaper effect is one story I've reflected upon for years. Armed with limited education my father was able to positively influence me tenfold.

There are many ways to observe the sandpaper effect. Sandpaper comes in various grades and types. It is a strong paper coated with a layer of sand or other abrasive, used for smoothing or polishing. After about the eighth time of rubbing my dad's hands it finally sank in. As an entrepreneur, I experience many days of fear and doubt; feelings we all experience periodically. The educational challenge for a child is simple: overcome this fear early and with practice it will become less crippling. Some say fear is only an illusion, something we create from within and this could be true. So in essence, _my father was smoothing or polishing away the fear_! He knew this would be the most important skill for me to learn when it became time for me to become my own boss.

Fun Parental Exercise:

Here's a fun way to highlight the power of choice in your child. You can use actual toys or pictures of toys or popular items the child may want. It may be best to use a picture so the child can see the benefits or rewards when they are able to obtain the items you're displaying. Take the child to a table and lay out a variety of pictures of these items. The key is in the picture placement. In the first row, pictures can be placed side-by-side. Do the same in the second row, only space the cards slightly further apart. When both rows are filled take more pictures and place them further behind the first two rows, as though they are in the background.

Now have the child review the pictures and select what they really want. The object is for the child to learn that they can choose from among the pictures in the background as well. Most children will focus on the first two rows and if so this serves as a good teaching point to discuss their choice thought process. In life, we always have the option to do something different. If we don't like our jobs we can switch or create our own. The goal is to spark this realization early enough so that the child can practice and become familiar with this thought process. You can do this exercise numerous times especially with toddlers because they will learn quickly. If you do this exercise and they ask for something not shown or displayed you may have a budding CEO in your home!

This proved to be very beneficial for me as a child. When my father did odd jobs on the weekend I usually accompanied him at times. This was how I was able to make extra money. Every Friday night my dad would prepare me by giving me an overview of what had to be done on Saturday, which meant my Friday all-nighters of Nintendo game playing were shortened. When I was 10-years-old, I would wake up at 6 a.m. ready to head to work with my father. We did everything from pouring concrete, to cutting down trees, to building decks and gates on our neighbors' property. As you can imagine, this was very tiring and at times frustrating because I wanted to play with my friends instead of being made to wear lumberjack shirts and yell timber when each tree fell. My father was also a magician so I would ask at times why he didn't simply make the tree disappear and he told me he didn't do it so I would learn how to work hard for a day's pay. Of course this left me wondering if he could really make the trees disappear. He would never tell.

When illustrating a point with kids on being an entrepreneur, it's important to highlight the power of choice. Among the words young children use as their speech and vocabulary increase, besides mom or dad, are the words yes and no. Both words have a lot of power. My father simply taught me that I always have a choice and if I don't like the way things are going I was empowered to do something different. This is by far a very important skill for an entrepreneur especially during the developmental stage of a business when one is required to make tough decisions.

Even though she worked in an office for many years, my mother was also an entrepreneur. In addition to working out of the home and raising a family she still managed to launch a successful in-home day care center. It didn't take long for her to realize that you can't depend on a company to take care of you forever, so she did what she could to bring in extra income for the home. As a result of my parents' example I realized that I possessed the formula and inherent drive to run my own company and custom design my life. However, my training was far from over. Remember rule #1 – The Power of Choice? My mother was no different from my father (with the exception of softer hands) because she knew that I would have to think and continue to apply myself to be successful in life.

My mom's day care unknowingly provided me with an opportunity to interact with younger children, but not without what I, as a teenager, thought came at a price. Do you remember when you were younger; let's say 10 – 15 years old? At that age you were into playing and simply having fun. My neighborhood was no different. Our street was nicknamed L-block and while the L stood for Lloyd you could symbolically conclude that the true meaning was learning because this would be the platform for all my future ventures. The L-block was full of kids who loved being kids. We did everything from playing sports, to exploring business ideas, to looking for new girls to talk to on one of our famous "girl hunts" because that's where boys at that age tend to focus. Sometimes those hunts ended miserably because we were limited by how far we could travel from home before getting into trouble.

As mentioned, my mom ran the day care center and every day after school I endured what seemed like punishment to me: no playing on the block until I helped watch the kids and get them settled.

I've always enjoyed and loved working with children, but when they stood between kickball and Kool-Aid it became a serious problem. My mother was a tough boss and I didn't have much authority in determining what jobs I would do at the day care center, and much to my embarrassment I was soon changing diapers. While mom was in the kitchen preparing a snack or beverage I was responsible for entertaining a room of 2 to 5-year-olds. I created all kinds of silly games that had no meaning whatsoever, but it was enough to silence the cries and complaints until the food and beverages arrived. The end of the day brought the largest reward because all the parents had to pick up their kids by 5 p.m. and off to L-block I would go.

I didn't realize it at the time, but it was during this phase of my life that I learned how much fun kids can be. Since I was growing myself I saw similar traits in them.

2

THE DRIVE BEGINS

When parents have to work continually to put food on the table other luxuries such as toys and games become second and third place in a child's life. When I was a kid, my parents worked very hard to provide and while they did an excellent job of raising me, I always had the desire or drive for more. Of course, from the ages of 4 − 10 it's limited to the latest toys, favorite ice cream or snack. To this day, I claim to have had the best childhood ever.

Increasingly, it's becoming quite common to hear about crime, poverty, food shortages, natural disasters and diseases in the world. Somewhere within all of us lie the answers or solutions to most problems. Do you remember how free you felt when you were younger? Were you worried about bills or taxes? Regardless of whether you had a dollar and some pennies or lint in your pocket you felt like you could take on anything.

Children can absorb information like a sponge. When I was around 12-years-old, my friends and I always used our brains to get the next dollar or meal, and a few years later, driving lessons. If there was no cash we simply created opportunities to put cash in our pockets. Children all over the world need positive affirmation to reinforce how limitless their minds can be.

The L-block was made up of all types of personalities comparable to the average office in any company. The trick was doing what we could to keep things entertaining and exciting at the same time. The block wasn't that big and there were trees bordering the sidewalks so while privacy was in abundance, it limited what we could do. Age-range also played a big role due to the older kids being more mature than us. For example, my big brother and his friends were teenagers and getting close to driving age so they simply had different interests and were able to do more.

Each week I would learn a new skill from my non-paid day care job. When it comes to the amount of information they can retain children are amazing. I learned a lot from them by simply observing their personality traits and problem solving in the day care. By now, you're getting a sense that my youth consisted of day care lessons, L-block adventures, sandpaper bruises and weekend excursions in the world of construction.

The next lesson was a vital one, which led to rule #2 – ***Exposure!*** It's amazing what a person can learn when they allow their mind and heart to roam. Similar to cell phones, when roaming, we walk, go, or travel without a fixed purpose or direction. It doesn't mean we're clueless or uninterested, it just means we're keeping an open mind. I once read a phrase that has since become a permanent hallmark when it comes to business. It reminds me of my parents and I'll explain why. The phrase comes from Carl Ally, founder of Ally & Gargano Advertising Agency. The headline was intriguing:

ONLY KNOW-IT-ALLS NEED APPLY ...

"The creative person wants to be a know-it-all. He wants to to know about all kinds of things: ancient history, nineteenth- century mathematics, current manufacturing techniques, flower arranging, and hog futures. Because he never knows when these ideas might come together to form a new idea. It may happen six minutes later or six months or six years down the road. But he has faith that it will happen."

It truly amazes me how my father could have had such a wealth of knowledge with limited education, no formal training nor advice from an educated person. It was something he'd learned the hard way and he was brilliant enough to teach it to his son by simply using things he knew would have a lasting impact on me whether I was 14 or 44. As parents, it's our desire to give our children the best life imaginable, and while not handing it to them on a silver platter, we hope they will someday understand and really get the point. Some parents may guess or wonder and some may never know, but with each stroke of the keyboard I'm living testimony that it does happen.

Exposure is another vital skill for children as they continue to develop and grow and I certainly didn't lack in this area. I grew up in a very small city (Chester, PA) outside of Philadelphia with a population slightly over 36,000. My father's routine never changed and he was well-known due to his work ethic. While riding in his truck to the next job he would always honk his horn at each corner. When I asked him why so many honks he simply said everyone knew him and although he didn't know them all by name there was some connection. There weren't too many things my dad didn't know when it came to construction. He would drive home the point that the more he was exposed to the trade the more obstacles he could overcome when it came to complex jobs.

The same would apply to me later in life. He always made it a point to make sure I talked to those we did jobs for because everyone came from different walks of life and you never knew what you could learn. This was also evident in my father's fascination with the nature channel. If there was ever a routine he had, it was watching what we called the "animal pictures" each night on our only TV in the living room. I never quite understood why he watched them so much, but I soon realized the importance of them and why exposure was critical when it came to developing the skills needed to be an entrepreneur.

One night there was a certain program I wanted to watch. Around 8 o'clock he came home, made his way to the living room where I was watching my show and asked, "What time does my animal picture come on and what channel?" Since he was pulled from school in the second grade he never learned to read, so I looked the TV guide over and told him nothing was on that night.

I was in the clear, or so I thought. As I sat there watching my show a commercial came on and my dad took the remote and slowly clicked through all the channels. Sure enough there was an "animal picture" on that night and once he realized I lied, I was rewarded with a one-week punishment. As if that weren't enough, I had to tell my friends what

I did to deserve the punishment, which only added to my embarrassment.

I never quite understood why exposure was important as a kid until one day when it all came together. My father and I were in the yard early one evening doing work when at least a dozen wild birds flew over us. My father stopped in the middle of his work and proceeded to call a wild bird. At first I thought my dad was going crazy, until one of the birds flew down to his hand and relaxed as if it was a trained parakeet or other house pet. He took the bird into the house to show my mom and upon seeing the wild bird; she may have thought it was attacking my father because she went ballistic.

The bird became equally nervous and agitated in reaction to my mother and immediately flew away. As if the first occurrence was barely believable my dad proceeded to call the bird and it flew back to him *again*. He then took it back outside and let it go. Amazed at what he did, I asked him where on earth did he learn how to call wild birds and without skipping a beat he said "the animal pictures". So again, exposure was key because my dad would always say you never know when things will come together for your own survival or to create income. He asked if I got the point and I nodded emphatically, all the while thinking to myself, "I wonder if that works on girls?"

Goal setting can be an easy or tough task depending on how we view them. Kids are reward-driven and I was no different. I was always seeking the next opportunity or way to convince my parents to buy me what I wanted. In my teens, I acquired another poster that had what would eventually become my favorite saying: "A goal is a dream with a deadline." So with the second rule under my belt (exposure), I proceeded to do all I could to become interested in whatever was thrown my way. I didn't jump for joy to watch animal pictures or anything, but I was aware. So aware that later in life one of my jobs involved pest control. There I was ridding people's homes of unwanted guests. While it wasn't the most glamorous job it was a great learning experience.

There are so many ways to make money and my father fell into the service category. He was a skilled laborer who could build a home from the ground up. The sandpaper effect taught me that there are other ways that included products or information, or what I refer to as the how-to's of the world. I would scan my room for old toys or books; anything I could rent to other kids or even my sisters. Whatever it would take, I was determined to have my own cash.

Fun Parental Exercise:

Exposure is another vital skill as your budding CEO continues to progress. We've all asked children the popular phrase what do you want to be when you grow up? This can be difficult for a child because at that point they may only be familiar with what they see on TV, and unless they aspire to be Big Bird or Barney there aren't many things they've been exposed to. This brings on the next fun venture, vocational role playing.

To do this it will require additional items such as clothing or uniforms so you can really give them the fun experience. To most kids it'll be like Halloween all over again so there should be no complaints. Think of all the different things a person can do, from being a doctor, firefighter, professional baseball player or even an actor/actress. The goal is to have your child simulate being that person. Granted, it may take some time for this to sink in, but it's a great way to help your child discover that inner talent they've been hiding. For example, let's say your child may want to simulate being a talk show *host. You can arrange the setting, have a fake microphone, use the family as an audience and give your child the stage. See how creative they may become by "running the show." Another example could be a famous artist. Kids typically love to draw, so you could have them put together some of their best paintings to auction. For the auction you can invite family and friends over and set up the room like an art gallery. The kids can even price their own work, at least until they ask for thousands of dollars for one piece! Not only will this continue to spark the drive, but it will also be great bonding for the family. Don't be surprised if your child starts demanding vocational role playing.*

As the days went by, I continued to tap into my resources to see what I could create. My dad knew what he was doing, and although I was labeled a devil-child at times, one day I would finally get it.

3

THE L-BLOCK LEMONADE STAND

Once the hunger developed I knew there would be no turning back. I was still relatively young and the lessons I learned from my parents about hard work, discipline and resourcefulness further molded me. When I should have been sleeping, I stayed up nurturing visions of me walking into the store and buying my first video game with my own money. It was still a challenge to think of the next plan, but you couldn't tell me anything different as I knew this was going to happen. It was just a matter of time. I found it hard to focus because the more I became exposed to different things the more I wanted to do. As an entrepreneur your weakness can also be your strength.

My bank of wealth lay in my ideas. Napoleon Hill wrote a book titled "Think and Grow Rich" and it's one I recommend all children (when they're older) and adults read. The more ideas I had the more flooded and cloudy my head felt. I knew I had to isolate my thoughts and think of the best way to move forward. I was never that great with details so I tried to surround myself with others who were. I could rattle off 10 different ideas, but if you asked the details I'd simply scratch my head and hope someone else spoke up.

The L-block was full of opportunities because of all the children, parents and neighbors available. I didn't read about lemonade stands in books nor did I see them on TV. The idea simply arose by observing the environment. We lived across the street from a middle school that had a track. On Saturday and Sunday mornings people would walk on the track for exercise. Our street provided direct access to the track. One particularly hot summer day I observed this scene and the light bulb went off.

I quickly recruited my best friend to figure out a plan for us to generate our next money-making venture. There's a saying that past performance is the best indicator of future success and that was true because when we made our first dollar selling lemonade we knew the sky would be the limit. The beauty of it all was the simplicity involved. We used our parents' glasses, Kool-Aid packets, sugar and water. The prospect of 100% profit was exciting because we had limited expenses.

Next, we had to determine the location, and as we know, location is everything. After carefully observing the joggers using the track and recording the frequency with which they passed by, we decided to use the front end of the street for our stand. It's tough to turn kids down especially when they take initiative, so we prepared our eager faces to display a careful blend of desperation softened by friendly smiles. We anticipated the excitement that would come from hearing the coins hit the registers and seeing the dollar bills fill the cash drawers as we collected payment from each dehydrated runner. This would be perfect, and we would rake in enough money to buy whatever our hearts desired, or so we thought.

Now that we had the location our next goal was to find the supplies needed to build the stand. We searched for hours to find pieces of wood. We checked behind schools, in dumpsters and parks. It was a firm lesson in determination for us because giving up was not an option. After a few days of coming up empty handed another light bulb went off. With my dad being in the construction field and doing odd jobs from time to time, the Inspector Gadget in me arose. I snooped around the back of his dump truck *et voila*, there were all types of scrap wood from what I believed to be leftover from jobs. They could have been materials for a new job, but nothing was going to stand in the way of my first company and the profits that would soon follow.

We eagerly grabbed the pieces of wood and whatever else we thought we would need. I got the nails and hammer from my basement and we began to assemble our first stand. We were young and not as strong so you can imagine how sturdy the stand was but that was the least of our concerns. Our priority was the cash and once we had enough we could upgrade and buy a coffee table or something. We went so far as to think that upon seeing our initiative and drive our parents would also contribute to help us purchase a better table. If they did we planned to offer them stake in the company.

Upon completion of our stand we were now ready to host but we still lacked the necessary supplies. There was a stand but that was it; we had no cups, fruit, sugar, Kool-Aid or cash register to hold the money (the most important item). My best friend and I both had a few siblings so groceries were scarce, but we managed to take (not ask for) all the supplies needed from our respective kitchens. Again, we knew the potential trouble we would be in, but by the time our parents would realize the shortage we would buy more supplies and offer them additional stake in the company.

The next crucial step would be running the stand. Flavor choices became the next item of concern as we only had the types of Kool-Aid that were available in our cupboards. We decided that thirsty people aren't that picky, so we sold the only flavor we had, lemonade. With limited Kool-Aid flavor options, we decided to offer penny candy as another product for sale. We know most people liked having a choice so the candy would be a good add-on to the stand.

There was nothing close to the mention of a recession so we assumed everyone would be willing to spend what we asked which led to the most important factor, pricing. We knew people would be more likely to buy if the price was reasonable, so 50 cents was the asking price. Our launch date was set and the next sunny Saturday would be the opening of the L-block lemonade stand. There was no ceremony or cutting of the ribbon, but we were determined to sell lemonade whether people were thirsty or not. So there we were on a Saturday early afternoon. To our benefit it was hot and humid and we received our first customer.

He was a runner and, as we expected, he was coming from the track. It was exciting to watch someone truly enjoy the refreshing beverage we'd prepared. It was not too long after that we learned our first lesson in customer feedback. He explained that we should probably purchase paper cups instead of plastic ones. Because resources were limited, we used the hard plastic cups from my friend's kitchen and we would simply wash them after each use. At first we felt it was a success but after a few customers said the same, we decided to scrounge up the money for the cups.

We now had our Grand Opening and after our first day of profit we soon realized we couldn't continue to use our parents' resources, we had to purchase our own. After an entire afternoon of running the stand we realized we didn't have any time to play or have fun on the block so the next day we acquired three employees, my little sister and her two friends. This would lead to rule #3 – ***Being a Manager!***

We paid them to run the stand while we played kickball, baseball and any other sport we wanted but that soon faded when they threatened to walk away and stop working the stand. It was a quick lesson in management and how to properly delegate duties while rewarding employees. Despite only making a few dollars we realized we did something special. We created a money-making venture simply by acting on our idea. Had we never thought of selling the lemonade there would have been no money.

I tell these stories for two reasons: 1) to highlight how money-making opportunities were easily available and 2) to show how a child's self-esteem can skyrocket when they accomplish something of monetary value, especially at a young age. I say monetary because it's not expected of a child to bring in income but when that happens something exciting occurs. They discover the power of thinking and problem solving. Who's to say the next inventor or person to cure AIDS or cancer is not your child. The possibilities are endless and while some may feel this is far-fetched, many successful creations began with a simple idea. A single, seemingly far-fetched thought, can be the creative spark that evolves an invention to change the world and how we think.

Fun Parental Exercise:

Training a kid to <u>be a manager</u> can be a daunting task. Most kids have very low attention spans and this can be a huge challenge. One way to explore this would be giving the project or challenge they have to oversee. For this example we'll use the idea of a plant. You can use something that's easy to grow or even the Chia Pets we've seen on the infomercial some years back. The idea is for the child to oversee the project from start to finish experiencing the rewards of seeing the plant grow. The goal is to pick something easy enough where the child can see the benefits quickly. Fruits and vegetables can also be fun as they will enjoy eating something they've grown and managed.

My father also owned a few gardens that were close to home and very convenient for my mom so we didn't have to buy many vegetables. The numerous trips to cultivate the garden taught me many lessons in people and project management. Although I was only 12 at the time, I could understand the importance of not over- watering plants or picking tomatoes too soon or too late. The same skill sets are easily transferable to the business world, especially when it comes to opportunities or important business decisions. In essence, we're providing our children the training without them knowing what it may be for or when it will impact them directly. My dad tried to make it as fun as possible without going overboard.

Of course it's never only about the money, but most if not all problems today have some form of financial attachment. Parents are stressed because of bills and making ends meet. While a struggle, children may observe these things and start to believe they're the norm when in actuality they are only temporary and depend on each person's situation. We're taught either directly or indirectly how to make money. If a child starts to tap into their entrepreneurial drive at a young age the cycle will continue and the hunger will grow deeper as they get older and become wiser.

I believe an entrepreneur is a person willing to take a risk producing something that will make a profit. As explained in previous pages, most kids are raised with the notion that failure is bad and that it should be avoided at all costs. Some schools today have modified their assessment methods and have adopted a grading system that uses numbers instead of letters. Most kids are smart and realize when they've failed but this shows how the educational system tends to shy away from children learning about failure. For some kids this can have a reverse effect almost to the point that a child concludes "Why should I try when I may fail?" No one wants to be a failure so some give up and don't try at all.

Just look to the left or right of you at work, school or at home. Many of the people you know among your family, friends and neighbors probably have wonderful ideas that could be very profitable. So what stands in their way? Is it the fear of accomplishing everything they set out to do? Being successful beyond their wildest dreams? Is it the fear of their children looking up to them and not being able to follow in their shoes given all the success they've had? NO! One key word is accurate in both statements and that's FEAR. It's natural and we all have it. The question is how do we deal with and overcome it. No matter what would happen in my life the sandpaper effect was always there, almost propelling me to continue to move forward.

Imagine if you were able to spark that drive in your child. What would his/her world be like? Would they cure cancer, solve the world's food shortage problems or even assist the government in somehow ending all wars for good? It seems far-fetched, but it's definitely within reach. Kids just need to know they can do anything if they continually apply themselves. There was a famous Addidas commercial that uses the tagline: **Impossible is nothing!**

As parents, we may, at times, face self-doubt and while it is a challenge we need to do what's best to not let our children start to believe that it can never happen or they will never be successful. Self-defeat is very contagious and can be detrimental to a child's development. So how can we prepare our kids for whatever comes their way? One word: focus.

4

YOUR FOCUS BECOMES YOUR REALITY

Have you ever met an optimistic person? How about the opposite? From time to time we encounter people from different walks of life. Optimist vs. pessimist. Good vs. bad. Light vs. dark. It's the constant struggle that becomes a part of life. Every day brings new decisions, choices and attitudes. When was the last time you had a conversation with someone who was negative to the tenth degree? How did it make you feel afterwards? Now think, was it a child or a teenager? It's one thing to talk to an adult who may be overwhelmingly negative, but when that person is a child or teenager it raises many eyebrows. I'll explain why.

As adults, we tend to rationalize why that person may be negative. Perhaps the individual was a product of their childhood upbringing or a traumatic experience. Rationalization makes it tolerable, although it may still unsettle us if an adult exhibits such an attitude, but when the negative person in question is a child the impact can be greater. We may start to wonder what is occurring in the life of a person so young that it causes them to be negative and self-defeating. This problem can escalate if we fall into the pessimistic category as this can have a major influence on our kids as we attempt to prepare them for adulthood. If you're not familiar with pessimism, observe the conversation/illustration below and try and fill in the blanks with someone you may know.

The setting: *Jane is a parent of two who works in social services. She's been in the same position for the past 10 years. Her good friend Tasha works with her and has been with the company the same amount of years. The following conversation is one that takes place daily. Their children hang out* *together and they also occasionally vacation together. See if you can pick out the negative and positive traits in each.*

Jane (arriving at work): Hey Tasha, how are you this morning?

Tasha: *I'm doing well, traffic was a little hectic, but I made it in safe, how about you?*

Jane: *I guess it's OK. My alarm clock went off late so Tim must have forgotten to set it again. That's all I need — another late day before being reprimanded.*

Tasha: *Well at least you made it in to work safe and unharmed. With this recession at full blast it's good to know we still have a job, you know?*

Jane: *Well, knowing me and my last performance they'll probably look to let me go because you know Human Resources just laid off 10 people. I really wanted to go back to school to finish my business degree, but Tim wasn't working at the* *time and now with the kids it's too hard to do it part-time. I just hope I'll be eligible for unemployment when they cut my position.*

Tasha: *Girl, you talk as if it's already been determined. Besides, you've been the go-to person on most projects around here the past two months. That's a big deal.*

Jane: *That's true but Stephanie (their manager) is probably doing that to give me a few last chances before they determine who goes and who stays. I just can't afford to be laid off right now. I've been checking the unemployment website to find out the criteria. They even list the max amount you can receive and it's based on your salary when laid off.*

Tasha: *Have you already received your pink slip? You talk as if you've been given a date already.*

Jane: *I haven't, but I noticed the way Stephanie talked and looked at me during our last meeting. She gave me a look as if my days were numbered.*

Tasha: *We talked yesterday morning and she was just getting over the flu so I'm sure she wasn't feeling the greatest. Just keep plugging away and everything will be fine. Well, I'm going to grab a coffee, would you like something?*

Jane: *Yes, can you get me a large sugar-free hazelnut soy latte. And can you make sure the coffee clerk uses the large cups? The last time he gave me two small ones because he said they were out of large cups. He probably didn't feel like getting them. People are always so negative and unhelpful these days.*

Tasha: *Will do Jane; don't cause any fires while I'm gone.*

Does that conversation remind you of anyone you know? While that conversation may seem humorous it's a common problem in most adults. Jane and Tasha displayed two important attitudinal traits we discussed earlier: pessimism and optimism. If we were to dissect the conversation it wouldn't be hard to see the differences in each. From the initial greeting to the closing statement Jane had nothing but negative things to say. Tasha, on the other hand, always countered with something positive. It's always good to have friends like Tasha, but what happens when both people are negative or difficult to deal with? This brings us to rule #4 – ***Establish a routine!***

Ultimately, we become what we think we are. Children are very observant and can pick up on negativity and the effect it can have on people. When we look at history, we see countless examples of individuals who chose to think nothing but positive thoughts or focus on what they aspired to be, not their current situation. The same rules apply today. If your child wants to be the first to discover life on another planet, who's to say he/she won't get there. The following examples illustrate how nothing can become something.

Who's ready to fly?

Wilbur and Orville Wright were two Americans credited with inventing and building the world's first successful airplane. Today, air travel is a popular mode of transportation. For more than a century, children have grown up familiar with planes and its perks. But when the Wright brothers first conceptualized their idea of making the ability to fly accessible to man, it came at a time when such thoughts were unheard of and the mere mention of "flying" was absurd.

So what did the Wright brothers have that we don't? Did they come from wealthy families who gave them everything? Did they have a world of supporters rallying them on as they sought to create the first plane? The answer to all the questions is a resounding NO! It was their focus that kept them on the right track. Both brothers attended high school, but neither graduated. Wilbur was planning to attend college but it never came to fruition, instead he looked after his sick mother and read numerous books in his father's extensive library. Orville also dropped out of high school to start a printing business, one his brother eventually joined. Next, they opened a repair and sales shop and this sparked their interest in flight. After repeated research they launched their first prototype and the rest is history.

The rodent that changed it all ...

Continuing with our observation of the importance of focus, let's explore the world of a man who was no overnight success. When we mention the words Disney to our kids many are familiar with the grand theme parks and characters that have redefined the cartoon industry.

Many know of the characters but most don't know the story behind the man, Walt Disney, after whom the magical wonderlands are named. Due to family problems as a child, Walt drew imaginary characters to pass time. Similar to the Wright brothers he was very ambitious and started a business as a teenager by creating the character "Oswald the Lucky Rabbit." Those cartoons became a big hit and Walt sold the characters to Universal Studios. Walt also signed away ownership of his creation so when it was time to renew his contract

Universal Studios declined. What would you do at that point? Imagine the feelings of frustration Walt felt as he no longer owned his main character. So what did he do? He began to refocus and went back to work. If he'd come this far there was no way he would give up now.

Walt thought back to when he worked in his uncle's garage. Sometimes we have to step back and reassess things before moving forward. The garage was infested with mice and Walt found a new friend and named him Mickey. Did Walt let the setbacks and potential negativity affect him? No. He simply kept moving forward. Had he not remained focused and driven none of his dreams would have come to fruition.

Fun Parental Exercise:

<u>Establishing a routine</u> may seem like a difficult task but it's easier than you think. Children will be able to focus better if their daily routine is the same. A critical piece to the sandpaper effect was the amount of times my father did it. Once he introduced the concept he would do it over and over again until I finally got it. Most kids go through what I call the "parental hero phase" in which they believe their parents can do anything. In other words they look up to them. While

at a training once, the instructor used this as an icebreaker. When talk show hosts enter the main area or studio a long uproarious applause awaits them. Sometimes this lasts for a minute or two. To help kids with establishing a routine why not have them coordinate cheering on a member of the family who they think has done something that deserves congratulations or recognition. In this way, the child can also learn how to encourage those around them. Of course this can be filtered and modified as time goes on, but the point is teaching the child that routine. Other methods can be used also but this is just a sample.

There are many other things we can use to help our children focus. Children are visual. This can be used to your advantage to help them find focus. You can use these aids to help when transitioning to another area of the house. For example, to get a kid to respond to dinner time you could play one of their favorite songs to let them know it's time to eat or the same can be done with playtime (although this may not work when it's time for bed as few children look forward to bedtime). Visual reminders are key to help them focus. Posters and art can be used. This allows parents to use non-verbal methods to encourage action in their children. They simply can look at the poster or sign and remember the task behind it. Talents are discovered at many phases of childhood; the key is exposing your child to enough of them to allow them to prosper. Just think of the many stories of famous people who knew what they wanted to be at a young age. We can't help but think of people like Tiger Woods who started playing golf when he was a toddler. It was all because of being exposed to the sport. Once he focused and established a routine it became gradually easier.

5

CUTTING GRASS FOR CHEESE FRIES

Does money grow on trees? My best friend and I pondered that question as we worked on our next business. The L-block lemonade stand brought in close to $10. Hungry from the taste of our first profit we felt the need to make more money in a shorter amount of time. It always amazes me how quickly a child's wants will change. One day it's a Barney toy, the next it's Big Bird and so on. We were no different, but now that we had our taste of business and the thrill of creating something from nothing we were hooked.

The amount of money made was never as important as being able to generate it. Money is simply an idea. We may have only made 75 cents with one venture, but during that time 75 cents was all we needed to buy the best cheese fries on the block. Yes, I remember it clearly. A pile of steaming hot french fries sandwiched between two slices of American cheese, one in the middle and one on top. Things were simple for most kids in my neighborhood and we all loved food. McDonald's provided instant gratification for our taste buds, but cheese fries were not popular or even available at most fast food restaurants in our area. There were only a few stores in the city that carried them and one was a stone's throw from L-block. It was still summer so the timing couldn't have been better. The L-block was full of parents who worked hard and wanted to relax on the weekends, therefore, if they could pay a small fee for good service it would be a win-win scenario. This created another opportunity for us to clean yards and cut grass. The plan was devised. We would charge $5 per lawn. That left us with $2.50 each for cheese fries. As for gas, we would borrow our parents' lawnmowers; so again, with no money out of our pockets we felt it was 100% profit.

The pitch to my father was very strategic. I had him feel my hands first to see how smooth they were. They were soft because I used my head to conjure up the next venture for spending money. I told him that in order to keep learning I had to do some hard work so I'd never take things for granted. He agreed and I borrowed all the other supplies we needed. There were still a few dollars left from the L-block lemonade stand so we used that for gas. Once my dad handed over what we needed from his truck I was struck with rule #5 – ***Leverage!***

To be an entrepreneur one must understand the importance of leverage. I describe leverage as something that occurs when one uses people, resources and technology to increase production for a desired result. Again, this refreshed the sandpaper effect emphasizing its effectiveness.

Just think of any large corporation such as Kimberly-Clark Corporation, which makes SCOTT® paper towels or Coca-Cola. For Kimberly-Clark to produce their multiple products each year, it requires a system of people, technology and resources to achieve their goals. Everyday items also demonstrate the power of leverage. Computers, cell phones, cars and leaf blowers are things we buy to help make things easier. Remember what life was like before cordless phones? It was impossible to be mobile; instead you were limited to the length of the phone's extension cord.

At the time, my friend and I didn't understand that what we were doing was demonstrating the execution of leverage. It was simply an innate ability that was cultivated through my father's frequent application of the sandpaper effect. We were now ready to start marketing our services. Instead of creating glitzy flyers we decided to have other neighbors speak for us. Word of mouth is arguably more influential than any other form of advertising. You can do direct mail, Internet advertising, even tradeshows, but people are more likely to believe what their friends and neighbors say about you and your services. We offered a discount on the first few lawns. We rotated cutting and raking each lawn. After we completed the first few jobs we encouraged our clients to tell their neighbors and friends about our services. As time went on we simply had to point out a lawn we did and let the visual provide the marketing we needed. It was our first lesson in hard labor and after a day of cutting grass our hands were sore, we were dirty, but we were still looking forward to starting another venture.

We made an average of $20 each Saturday, enough for cheese fries and a movie. My dad was proud, so proud he felt he no longer had to give me lunch money but that didn't last long because I spent more than I made. Business was booming and the beauty of it all was two words: repeat customers. Once we signed on a new neighbor as a client we agreed to cut their grass every weekend until the winter. Most were happy to accept because this freed up their Saturday and we could count on a certain amount of cash. At this point, we successfully launched two businesses in a relatively short period of time. The profits were small but the lessons learned were invaluable.

Fun Parental Exercise:

So how can you teach or show your child the importance of <u>leverage</u>? While there may be many ways the thing to remember is simplicity. Kids are very simple and they know the true meaning of "less is more." Of the many words they learn, the more frequently used are "yes" and "no." Reflecting on the definition used earlier, the goal is to show him/her the power of leverage and how they can use it to their benefit. There's a show on TV called "Hoarders" which follows people who accumulate things and can't let go. Eventually this can become hazardous depending on the situation. While children may not be as bad they can accumulate lots of toys. Between birthdays, holidays and any other celebrations, it's no surprise how quickly things add up. Try giving your child the option to "upgrade" their toys. For example, let's say the child's birthday is months away and no holidays are close. If there is an item they really want allow them to make a trade by turning in toys that could be equal to the value of the item they want. You could even take the toys they trade in and have them donate them to charity or Toys for Tots. This also allows children to see the benefits of charity and giving. Eventually they'll attempt to trade in at any chance they get so be careful. Leverage is a powerful tool and can be used in any situation. By helping them see the importance involved it will further prepare them for their future.

6

Shoveling Snow for Hot Chocolate

How many times have you heard "Money can't buy happiness?" It's a popular adage many people use and they have good reason. We do need money to buy and sell things but it's not the end result. A verse in the Bible also states that money is for a protection. The goal is to understand and observe how we view it. When we're young it may have taken some time to truly understand the value of money and its importance. Can it truly make you happy though?

Did you know it's one of the most researched questions of all time? People go to great lengths to discover the accuracy of the statement. Studies all over the world take place to understand the validity of the phrase. Some say it's all in the eye of the beholder, others claim it depends on how much but what is the magic answer and how did this affect my friend and me as we worked on our next company. There are pros and cons to any scenario and this one is no different. Our parents and those surrounding us were perfect subjects to observe in our environment because we could examine the differences in how money was valued among those who had and those who hadn't.

There is one thing no human being can escape. It's a four-letter word, starts with a T and ends with E. You guessed it, TIME! Most of us have daydreamed on occasion and in those dreams we create an imaginary lifestyle, pondering what we would do if we had more money than we needed. Some would sail the ocean, others would maybe buy a restaurant or franchise and others still would find ways to make more. If we reflect on the things we do that require time we can see how quickly our days fill up. Caretakers, assistants, personal chefs and trainers are all available to do the things that will give us more time. Of course they cost money so the average household can't afford to pay for all those things. So the pros would be more time to do whatever we please.

But what's the negative? Some say it can be simple, others say it's more complex. For the sake of this book we'll keep it simple. Most of us enjoyed the independence that came with adolescence as we outgrew childhood. We became busy and we liked having to do lists and responsibility. Some may feel lazy or inadequate if everything was paid for and they didn't have to lift a finger. For most the pros will outweigh the cons, but it's something to consider.

As kids, this began to sink in for us; the sandpaper effect realized again. It would take lots of work and patience to accumulate wealth. We'd heard of get-rich-quick schemes as kids but we were smart enough to know the odds and how often it really happened. Many celebrities, actors and athletes understand that hard work and patience is needed to succeed. In other words they worked at it and became the best in their trade. The more practice the more the fear would fade away. Each rub of the sandpaper made me stronger and my willpower grew.

So what else did we observe? Ah, the accumulation of material goods. Anything can fall in to this category: toys, food, traveling, cars, clothes, etc. Most reason that if they only had this or that they could purchase the car or home of their dreams in an attempt to gain complete satisfaction which would presumably lead to happiness. With that said, can there be a downside to having too many material goods? From childhood through adulthood, we all have to tendency to wear things out and we eventually want something new or better. As kids, my friends and I were certainly aware of this. As proof, all we had to do was look around at the toys that had been quickly discarded in favor of the new one we received with the arrival of Christmas or a birthday. By the time the next big day rolled around, however, the previous year's toys were history.

As we reflect on the title of this chapter it becomes obvious what our next venture would be.

No matter the season we were determined to keep exploring to keep the time going, unaware that these principles had the potential to set us free for life. At first glance it all seems so basic, but when the snow comes along with freezing temperatures there's nothing better than a hot cup of chocolate topped with whipped cream. We loved video games and watching movies in my friend's basement, so hot chocolate would be the perfect compliment as we watched Ace Ventura for the fiftieth time.

Similar to when we launched our lawn mowing business, we realized that the L-block was ripe for the picking and there was always competition from neighboring kids. As we went back to the drawing board to figure out supplies I was struck with rule #6 – _**Repetition!**_ We were sitting there attempting to come up with new customers and realized there was no need to do that. We received great reviews from our neighbors who were existing clients. Therefore, we could simply tap into that existing customer base to market our new business of snow removal from sidewalks and driveways.

We got a lot of satisfaction from shoveling. My father's resistance to provide supplies gradually weakened as he saw my entrepreneurial drive increase. He knew the sandpaper effect was working. Once we were all geared up we headed outside. Neighbors could sense our new-found self-confidence. No longer were we dependent on their kindness, begging for new business, and our reputation and professionalism spoke volumes about our services. We realized that fear was something we had complete control of and once that vanished all that was left was success.

The end result was numerous driveways and sidewalks paved to perfection. Our reward was the simple pleasure of sitting in my friend's basement playing games, eating grilled cheese and enjoying endless cups of hot chocolate.

Fun Parental Exercise:

Repetition can be one of the easier exercises for kids. Think back to the time they made their first attempt to walk. They fell countless times but what happened? They got back up, fell, maybe endured some soreness or even cried. Despite the disappointment they kept trying, and when they finally reached a few steps or two the joy far outweighed the dissatisfaction of falling. Suddenly they had renewed vigor and kept walking, perhaps holding your hand until they eventually walked on their own. At times my weekends consisted of visiting my grandfather in Delaware. It was the best of times. He would take us to McDonald's or Burger King (we always chose McDonald's) for breakfast and we'd play all afternoon. My grandfather would always tell us to relax if we couldn't get something or got frustrated. As kids the last thing we wanted to do was relax but it worked. When we sat down to relax and enjoy a refreshing glass of my grandmother's lemonade, we were much more prepared to go back to the problem we encountered. This method can be easy to implement. To make it fun, try this: take three playing cards with pictures and shuffle them starting slow and eventually going fast. Show them the picture you want them to guess out of the three. Make the first few tries easy so they can guess the right picture and then speed up the process until they can't keep up and start getting the incorrect one. As they become a little frustrated have them do something fun and active like jumping jacks. Then have them relax and go back to the cards. Start off at a medium pace and congratulate them each time they get the right card.

Anxiety and stress can be brutal when trying to learn or recall something. This takes place because our minds shift towards worrying instead of focusing on what's needed. If your attention is diverted it's no surprise that it will be a challenge to remember what's needed. The relaxation method will help kids while they're young and like the sandpaper effect they learn to cope and deal with the anxiety and stress that comes with life.

Many of us cringed when it was time to take the SATs or any major school exams; this was because of the pressure. Test anxiety can be very common in kids. In high school it was the same for me. I would know the material inside out, but when the teacher said "begin," I froze. Because of the time constraints, anxiety clouded the material I knew. I was more focused on the stress instead of the actual answers to the exams. The same can happen in the workplace, which can be very demanding. These can all be mitigated by repetition of this exercise. Imagine your kid encountering all types of problems with ease. It can happen!

7

Wanting to be like Mike

Do you remember being asked "What do you want to be when you grow up?" It's very common to have a purpose in life and children are no different. To them everything seems possible and if there's something they can't do, mommy and daddy can. We grow up believing our parents have the answers to everything because they're adults. As we get older we start to understand how they found those answers and how we can do the same.

But there's something else that can help us navigate those tough times. When we encountered challenges and disappointment we turned to role models. Why? Because they seemed to have everything we aspired to acquire. They were successful, well-known and popular. To clarify, role models come in different forms; they can be wealthy and famous or regular people whom we admire.

Observing their successes helped propel our desire to want to accomplish everything we set out to do. One of my role models was Michael Jordan.

He's regarded as the greatest basketball player ever to play the game. Early in his career you may have recalled that catchy jingle "Like Mike, if I could be like Mike." Every young basketball player in America and even the world wanted to be like Mike. For us on the L-block, it was no different because it was a way for us to escape, a way for us to put ourselves in his shoes to help us achieve our goals. This underscores the importance of role models. Is there a selection process? Should it be done formally or informally? The answer depends on the child. Role models help us become the person we aspire to be. This can be a challenging task for parents because just as there are good role models, there are bad ones also.

So how can you be a positive influence in your child's life so that they will choose a good role model? First, encourage your child to find someone who has a lot of confidence in themselves and their abilities. It doesn't have to be an athlete or famous person. In chapter 4 we looked at negativity. We should avoid a role model who could bring about negative thinking. They should also be around someone who's not afraid to be themselves. There are more than 6 billion people on earth and just imagine if even half of them were the same. What if they acted the same, ate the same food, drove the same cars, and lived in the same kind of homes. Does the term clone sound familiar?

The role model should also exhibit good social skills, and know how to interact well with others. Some may feel this is a challenge for a toddler, but remember some kids will follow in their parents' footsteps so if you set the expectation early on they may want to do the same. My father was constantly concerned about the friends I had. He knew the area well and in such a small city the bad sometimes outweighed the good. As I got a little older we would get into arguments and on one occasion the importance of role models really sunk in. He would always encourage me to be myself and not always follow others and this led to rule #7 – ***Be Unique!***

I never truly understood the effects of peer pressure until I went to middle school. I was 13-years-old and the sandpaper effect continued to mature. The school I attended was across the street from my home so you can imagine the repercussions if I ever got in trouble due to tardiness. In a school there are various types of populations and crowds and they all form what's called cliques. One of my weaknesses as a kid was always trying to please everyone. My father always taught me to have no enemies so my goal was to know everyone. This worked well initially, but eventually I got into trouble by simply following the wrong crowd. Once again my dad reinforced being unique and standing out in the crowd. It can be challenging as a kid because you want everyone to like you and no one likes the idea of being an outcast, but the sandpaper effect trained me well.

In business there's a term used in marketing that differentiates a company from its competitors.

It's called the Unique Selling Proposition (USP). Once again, my father was able to educate me not even knowing how to spell those words. He knew that by me being different and exploring all avenues I would create something no one could duplicate. When working on a new invention, company or product, the inventor breathes life into the product. It can be imitated or copied by others but the USP is what will set them apart from the others. What's even better is using your USP to fill a crucial void in the marketplace. So what did all this mean for my best friend and me, two kids who already started a few businesses before high school? It meant it was time for a new venture.

Reflecting on the amount of money we made at the time, some may now see it as a joke, but the lessons learned were more important than the profits we made. We knew that if we duplicated the same drive eventually fear would dissipate and we'd accomplish whatever we set out to do. It was now time for more research. In our school there were lots of girls and we were now in the phase of finding "the one" (so we thought). We used to play a game called "girl hunt" which consisted of going on walking tours (we were too young to drive) to find our future girlfriend. Now we understand why they looked at us funny as there were 4 or 5 boys hounding one girl in our respective quest to find "the one." While we failed miserably in our quest, we noticed one crucial point that would eventually be our next investment. All the girls in our school wore make-up and it was all about enhancing one's appearance to be noticed by others.

Our target market consisted of all girls ages 12 – 18 and adults, specifically our parents and their friends. What young lady could turn down two handsome gentlemen looking to enhance their appearance? That was our thinking and we were determined to launch the next venture. When it came to girls I didn't have much confidence as a teenager, but this next company helped break the ice especially when it came to conversation starters. Because money was the main motivator rejection was easy to handle because they weren't turning me down, instead I saw it as their reluctance to spend money on make-up. We already had a plan to offer free samples if they weren't interested. The vision, goals and strategy were all in place but we were missing one main thing: the product.

This would be a challenge because all our past ventures involved raiding our parents' cupboards for supplies and while my mom's vanity case was good for her, we weren't convinced a 13-year-old girl would use the same product. We also had limited start-up capital because there were no leftover funds from our previous businesses that we could use as seed money to purchase the make-up products. One day, as we scanned the classifieds we saw an ad for Avon, the world's largest direct sales beauty company. The ad sought independent sales representatives who wanted to take control of their careers and be their own boss. We were too young to think along the lines of careers, but we knew what being the boss was like. We enjoyed the satisfaction of prior businesses and the generated profits.

We contacted the company and within days the interview was set. We went in at the same time and the regional manager who interviewed us was very impressed with our level of determination. We were young entrepreneurs with dreams of securing multiple income sources. She went through the orientation and after providing us with a handful of supplies, brochures and order forms she pronounced us independent Avon consultants.

We received a certain percentage of all orders placed so the more we sold the more money we would make. We developed an oral marketing plan (we were too lazy to actually type something) to help keep us on track. We went through all the brochures and pamphlets to highlight what we felt were good buys. The key was finding out what our customers currently used so that we could direct them to something better. After bookmarking our pages we planned the launch date. Each new venture brought a fresh level of excitement I can't explain. You could say it was the rush; the idea of creating something from nothing. The products were supplied, but the business would have never taken off if there was no drive.

It was a clear day and we were armed with various creams and lotions, as well as our sales pitch. We walked all over the area pitching to our neighbors, relatives and friends. Some friends laughed because Avon is normally sold by women. It wasn't that there were no men who sold the products, it just wasn't the norm but rule #7 (Be Unique) kept me motivated. We actually had lots of fun as customers flipped through the pages placing various check marks for items they would purchase. Our confidence skyrocketed as we had to request more order forms to keep up with the high demand.

When we revisited the girls who were initially resistant to our sales pitch things changed and our orders steadily increased. Billions of dollars are spent on beauty supplies each year and sharing interesting statistics with our customers made the conversation more appealing. My ice-breakers were ironclad and the addiction grew as I became more comfortable. I remember telling one girl she had a beautiful smile but unless she further enhanced herself with the products we sold that was all she would have. It's no surprise that she became a regular customer. This would prove to be our most successful business. We worked so hard on our first day that we made a few hundred dollars in less than eight hours. Our desire for selling Avon declined and soon we were ready for the next venture. After all, we were kids so our attention spans shifted faster than a hummingbird's wings.

Fun Parental Exercise:

Being Unique is easily attainable once a child recognizes the benefits. At some point, most of us have fallen victim to peer pressure. It's important for children to understand and realize that being different is a "good" thing and they don't always have to follow what others do. This exercise is gradual as it will help your child to see their individual importance in the family and that their opinions matter. Most kids know no limits and depending on the number of kids in the family this exercise can be lots of fun. One way to encourage individuality in the family is "Special Days" or "Recognition Days". As kids become more independent they like to make decisions. As with any of the exercises mentioned throughout the book, there can be rules to the days. It's best to do it on a Saturday so the child can have full control. The special or recognition day are named after them. For example, it would be "Timothy's Day" or "Christina's Day" and they would be empowered to major decisions, such as what to eat for breakfast, lunch and dinner.

If they want to go to the movies or Chucky E Cheese's it's up to them and the family participates. If there are siblings one rule will be not picking what's already been done. This means they will need to do something different. Of course this can be modified as an entire day can be taxing for parents especially if there are many siblings. If so, you could just do one activity such as lunch or breakfast.

8

THE APPROACH: CAN YOU PLAY BASKETBALL?

By the time I was 16 the sandpaper effect was so engrained that I didn't let a day go by without exploring or seeking something new. My mind was open and I had many ideas and paths to pursue. We were now teenagers with a few businesses under our belt. Many professionals nowadays will tell you to plan for the future and live in the present not the past. Increasingly we see or hear of individuals who can't let go of things, or are so focused on the future that they don't see what's right in front of them. From the time I was a toddler I had goals and dreams and never let them die. Some I've accomplished and others are within grasp.

The L-block was full of children with passion and a drive to do whatever was considered fun. The ratio of boys to girls was even and there was never a shortage of games for us to play, including different sports. There were numerous playing fields across the street from L-block. It was our playground and a place for us to showboat our skills. From baseball, kickball, dodge ball, football and track each of us was determined to be the best at one of these. Organizing teams were never a problem because there were lots of kids to rotate. There was a basketball court in our back alley where we practiced. Some of my friends' parents were very involved and their kids had been playing basketball since middle school. Most of our days consisted of back-to-back games in the alley. If you ask me, they were really clinics because my friends were very good and I was just playing for fun. I had an OK jump shot and my height gave me additional advantages. We would have barbeques out back and play all day. Similar to the Kool-Aid commercials, halftime consisted of us raiding our parent's refrigerators to re-hydrate.

We would continue the fun until the street lights came on, which was our signal to head in for dinner. I had never played organized basketball so the thought of going out for the high school team was absurd. The terminology alone was foreign to me until one day that all changed. I was headed to my next class and the varsity basketball coach approached me. I greeted him with a nod as I kept walking. Seconds later he approached me and inquired, "Have you ever thought about playing basketball?" I told him about my daily battles on our alley court, but this hardly compared to playing official basketball. He laughed a bit and then proceeded to invite me to tryouts. He made me promise I would be there so there was no turning back.

When I went home I briefly talked to my dad about the coach's offer. After explaining the conversation I had with the coach my dad asked four questions:

Do you think you can play?

Do you enjoy playing?

Can you commit the time?

Will you be ready?

After the last question I knew this was another test. The sandpaper effect was implemented to erase my fears, so he knew each response would have three letters instead of two. That night I found myself staring out my back window at the alley court. It was late and I had so much on my mind so I took my ball and went out to shoot foul shots. I began to realize each milestone as the ball went through the hoop. In a few short hours I convinced myself I wouldn't be average and I would stand out and just like that I was struck with rule #8 – ***Ask Questions!***

It all started with my coach. He asked the question which planted the seed. My dad, in turn, did the same realizing this would ensure that I'd come to the conclusion myself. I was a little nervous, but I'd accomplish so much as a kid that I knew I would be a success even if I failed. While on the court that night I visualized everything from practice to game time. I heard my name being called as a starter, I saw me hitting my first basket, making my first block, throwing down my first dunk or alley-oop, hearing the cheering crowd as the adrenaline continued to flow and just like that I was snapped back to reality. I realized that what I had imagined to be an energetic crowd cheering and yelling my name was really my neighbor leaning out her window yelling at me to stop bouncing the ball at 2 a.m.

The next day I woke up a new man, ready to conquer the courts. Tryouts were a few days away and I told my friends what I was planning to do. They were all excited because they knew my potential. I was very humble due to inexperience, something my coach told me was key. There were a lot of guys going out for the team. I was only in the tenth grade so I barely made junior varsity. It was obvious that I had the energy, but lacked the theoretical background needed to be successful. In fact, the first game of my career the coach asked me to substitute for another player and I ran onto the court without letting the officials know I was coming in the game. As the crowd laughed I realized I had a long way to go but the sandpaper effect would never let me down. I wasn't scared, just unfamiliar to what was around me.

There were barely any stats the end of my sophomore and junior years because I was new and inexperienced. It was fun to play with so many talented guys but I never lost sight of my goal which was to be a basketball standout. The summer preceding my senior year proved to be my breakout phase. Prior to joining the basketball team my high school coach had a long heart-to-heart talk with me regarding my future. I had a 3.6 GPA and he knew I was very trainable. He explained that if I was serious about my goals I would have to play an entire summer of rigorous basketball which meant two things: 1) when I wasn't playing I would be practicing and 2) when I wasn't practicing I would be playing. It would be a full-time commitment, but with the drive that began in chapter 2 behind me it was a breeze mentally.

We played all summer long. There were at least three different leagues along with practice in between. Towards the end of the summer my coach saw the dramatic increase in my performance and skills. Before the start of the season we had another talk about my future goals. Again he proceeded to ask questions covering everything from colleges and cities to professions and scholarships. He encouraged me to use basketball as a stepping stone to get to my final destination. This reintroduced rule #5 (leverage) as I would be using my basketball talents to accomplish my goals.

The season was now ready to commence and each sport has their pre-season prediction when it comes to players and teams. I was unheard of as the previous two seasons proved to be uneventful due to my playing limited minutes with limited stats. I still remember pre-season clearly as we endured tryouts once again. By this point, I knew that this was my last shot to make a statement as one of my goals included college. It was a hot day in the gym and we were sweating buckets. As usual, there were a few slackers along with those who partied more than they played in the summer.

One day during our training we were doing double suicides. For those unfamiliar with basketball, a suicide is a cardiovascular drill that builds leg strength and endurance. You begin the drill at one of the baselines and run out to the foul line and then back to the baseline. Then you run out to half-court and back. Next, you run to the opposite foul line and back. Finally, you run the full court down and back. The goal is to run, not jog and we were doing doubles which meant back-to-back suicides without stopping. After the first two, the coaches were mad because they could tell some of the players weren't running and others were in poor shape. They made us all sit on the court. For 15 minutes we were verbally challenged. One of the coaches pulled rule # 8 (ask questions). The last three helped to make my name known. He said:

Do you know who's outworking everyone on
the court?
Is there anyone on the court better than him?
You want to know who's going to be a star
this year?

After these questions I had at least three to four guys in mind. You see, I played basketball in a city that produced players like Jameer Nelson (Orlando Magic) and Tyreke Evans (Sacramento Kings) so there was no shortage of talent. He concluded by saying one word: **MILSAP!**

There were no nods or signs of confirmation from the players because he had now struck a chord with everyone. He just created healthy competition. I partially feared for my spot because I knew others would now kick it up two notches to prove him wrong. It was actually what we all needed to keep going. I mentioned partial fear because it only lasted for a few days before I began to apply the sandpaper effect. It was my time and no one would take it from me.

We were now a few days from our opening tournament to start the season. The team was set and we were all fired up and ready to destroy the competition. My high school was always known for basketball so the games were packed and the defending school always had a hard time hearing plays due to all the noise. The day before the game we were playing around at the end of practice. We tried to do crazy shots like shooting from half court along with acrobatic dunks for those who could slam. I was 6' 4" at the time and my legs were strong – compliments of the double suicides. It was the end of practice and during horse play one of my teammates lobbed the ball from half court. I came from the right side, and with two hands caught the pass and threw it down. We were all amazed during practice and joked that we would do that in the game.

At game time we played a small school outside of Philadelphia. The adrenaline alone was enough to play six back-to-back games. A blowout was in the making and it was now time to give everyone a glimpse of how limitless our talents were. The play was similar to the one in practice and as our star guard dribbled down he saw me speed up as I approached the right side of the basket. It didn't matter if the coach would get mad because we would still walk away with the win. I was full of confidence and playing my first game with cheers instead of boos. I envisioned the passion I would display if we pulled it off. Without hesitating he launched the ball high in the air after crossing half court. There were a couple defenders running back so we weren't sure it would be complete. Seconds later I came out of nowhere, and with one hand I caught the ball from half court in the air and threw it down like there was no tomorrow. As you can imagine, the crowd went crazy and there was a pause entering the ball due to all the noise. From that point forward they knew a star had been born; something I already believed.

The next day in school you couldn't have a conversation without talking about the alley-oop we did. It was a major boost to our self-esteem (something needed as an entrepreneur). Asking questions allowed me to consider things I never thought I could attain. Local newspapers wrote about the fantastic play by our team, which brought us a lot of attention. Most of the articles included comments as if to say: "Who is this person?" I was a late bloomer, but every point scored increased my confidence and my goals would be realized.

Soon it was time for me to prepare for the next level: college. My uncle was influential in helping me get there. My father utilized his resources by having me follow my uncle's lead. My uncle kept me on track and made sure my books and grades were in order. As the year progressed I began the hunt for schools to determine which one I would attend. This was all new to me and my sister attended a college in Lancaster, Pennsylvania so I was able to visit from time to time. I fell in love with the campus and made a choice to go there despite all the big Philadelphia schools looking to recruit me. I truly believe everything happens for a reason so although I could have attended a Division I school, I never regretted my decisions.

After spending a semester in Lancaster things didn't go as planned and I ended up transferring to a college in upstate New York. My dreams were realized and I was now in college simply due to applying myself, asking questions and moving forward. I went on to become an All-American and my college coach taught me many things that I continue to use today. So when it comes to your child's progress encourage them by asking questions that challenge them to think. Anything worthwhile will take time to accomplish. Lack of self-esteem is the leading cause of many problems today when it comes to children and teenagers. Applying the sandpaper effect will enable your child to grow and erase many of their fears by continually applying themselves. College proved to be some of the best years of my life. It was the first time that I was on my own. Even though my parents were only six hours away, it was close enough to get home when I needed to. I still continued to work part-time and pursue small ventures to generate income to support myself at school.

Fun Parental Exercise:

None of us is perfect and the same goes for the most successful entrepreneur. They face and endure numerous trials on a daily basis. It's only through asking questions that they learn how to tackle these problems. The same rule applies to children. Once again, children are very inquisitive by nature and they have an ingrained desire to want to know more. If you don't agree simply answer a child's question and they will usually ask why. So how can you help your child to effectively ask questions (a needed trait for entrepreneurs)? You can start by thinking out loud. For example, if there's an answer you're seeking you can simply say out loud "I wonder why that happened?" By doing this regularly you'll begin to train your child to do the same. You can also encourage your child to ask and answer questions by applying themselves to the scenario. My father always loved the nature channel. Animals in the wild revealed many things to him. As a youth I was forced to watch them so I had no choice but to pretend to be interested. Most kids love animals so you could watch a special with them and when something's performed by the animal like: drinking water, or flying to a new location you can say "Hmmm, why do you think they're drinking that water?" or "Why did the bird fly away and return with food?" This will encourage your child to begin to always ask questions.

9

From $0 - $2,302

Some people believe wealth can only be obtained by those that are super smart. Others believe that it takes money to make money. Some are frustrated with trying to obtain it and a few actually feel you can have anything if you simply focus and don't give up. Life's experiences cause most of us to come to different conclusions that can end up determining our lot given the path we take. There's a scripture in the Bible that covers this very well. Proverbs 13:12 reads: "Expectation postponed is making the heart sick, but the thing desired is a tree of life when it does come."

Endurance is critical when it comes to achieving any goal and this can be the most challenging for a child. For most parents this is a very difficult task because some have given up on dreams and a few never set out to obtain them. I've read numerous books on personal success and one of my favorites is titled "Think and Grow Rich" by Napoleon Hill. It demonstrates how high achievement and financial independence can be obtained. The author was born into poverty but died a wealthy man. He never gave up and he believed each person's responsibility is to persevere and succeed in spite of obstacles.

It never dawned on me that much of what my father was teaching me was written about in books. Similar to Hill, I didn't come from wealth, but my father worked very hard to make sure we had the necessities. The previous eight rules helped solidify my quest for knowledge. Many dream of being wealthy but most don't realize the preparation involved in getting there. The by-product is money. While it is important, money shouldn't be the focal point because one stands the risk of becoming so consumed with acquiring it one can overlook critical details which could eventually sabotage your entire venture.

There's a popular saying: practice makes perfect, but have you wondered why it's so popular? Casual observation of history shows that successful people establish a pattern. Overnight success, with little or no work of preparation, is very rare.

I remember being 15-years-old and anxious to drive. Obtaining a license is a significant milestone in a teenager's life. My friends and I would daily watch different cars and periodically we'd identify the ones we hoped to have someday. To my father, driving was no big deal because he'd been driving since the age of 13. I wasn't the greatest test taker, but I always tried to visualize and dream what I wanted to happen. While preparing for my learner's permit I did everything I could to see myself driving and then I was hit with rule #9 – ***Constructive Imagination!***

The power of imagination is often underestimated. It's the ability to form a mental image of something that is not perceived through the senses. We all posses the ability to imagine, we just need to know how to tap into it. It can come in a variety of forms, the most popular being daydreaming. The beauty of it is the fact that it's limitless. You can go anywhere, be who you want to be and accomplish whatever's in your path. The key is bringing these visions to life. For an entrepreneur, it's about seeing the end before you begin.

As I got older I continued to explore various ventures until I found something I was good at. I pursued car auctions, multi-level marketing companies and even sold diet products. While I made money on some it always seemed I was paying more than expected. While some of my friends went on to have very successful careers in those fields, it simply was not something that worked for me.

In my early 20s I relocated to upstate New York. A few colleagues of mine were involved in creative real estate and this piqued my interest. I'd always heard of the many gurus doing deals with pennies. When you first hear of these you assume it's too good to be true as it always is. I decided to enroll in a course that taught the fundamentals on understanding and foreclosures. The biggest challenge would be convincing owners and banks

I knew what I was doing. Once again, imagination kicked in. I went to the courthouse, created a business name and printed my first foreclosure list.

I thought back to the days of driving and how I had to visualize success before it happened. The sandpaper effect was still in view. Below is a favorite quote of mine from Victoria Jackson, Founder of Victoria Jackson Cosmetics:

Visualize Your Success Story

"Act as if says it all. If you look like, sound like and visualize your success, you will come to know anything is possible. I used to visualize cosmetics coming off a conveyor belt with my name on the label. I could actually see the compacts being packed into boxes for shipment. I knew it would happen and I never took no for an answer. I learned from each failure and those failures became part of my success story that I knew I would tell one day. I never looked back but remained focused on my future. My future is here. Read your own success story and it will happen."

My training on foreclosures was complete and it was now time to put into practice what I learned. I was doing OK financially, but I wanted to do a deal that required a limited investment. A good friend and investor told me if I can learn to make money with no money I would be set for life. I started what's known in the business as farming neighborhoods. It's amazing how many things present themselves when your eyes are opened. I was looking for homes that looked vacant or rundown. I pursued various forms of advertising including: door-to-door knocking, flyers, signs and direct mail. After two days of searching I found a neglected home that was only two blocks from my house. The home had been vacant for six months and I didn't even notice.

Initially I tried to find contact information on the owner by searching the public records and asking neighbors. After three days with no response I decided to leave a note on the front door. I chose bright colored paper so it could stand out from the street. I included my contact information with a note that said: "I want to buy this house." That's all it took for the owner to call me the next day. I became a little nervous as he asked how many homes I've done in the past. To my surprise he appreciated my honesty and preferred to work with me because I was straight-forward and willing to ensure a deal was made with the bank.

A foreclosure transaction requires signing numerous documents. Some forms had tough questions and although it took me some time to answer them all the homeowner appreciated me not being presumptuous. When we completed the paperwork we contacted the bank. Similar to today, foreclosures are on the rise and some banks are so behind with these transactions that it can take up to 90 days to get an answer on a deal. The bank was very anxious as I dealt with loss mitigation. For those unfamiliar, loss mitigation is a division within a bank that mitigates the loss of the bank, or a firm that handles the process of negotiation between a homeowner and the lender/buyer. They are known to be very tough and completing deals aren't as easy as they appear in the textbooks. I was confident I would persuade them to see my point and allow us to purchase the home at a discount.

It took a few days for them to respond and in the interim I faced some negativity from others. This brings me to my next point when it comes to dreams and making things happen. As we all know, there will always be people around you who feel what your doing will never happen. Some said I'd never buy and sell a home without using any of my own money. Others laughed and shook their heads in disbelief. Its times like these that imagination really starts to take over. It was my first time working with loss mitigation and even if the deal fell through I would have continued going through the No's until the first Yes. Whatever your child may pursue, it's important to stress to them the importance of sticking to their goal and not letting others sway them from their dreams. People don't like to see others succeed because it reminds them of what they can't or are unwilling to do. Because they don't pursue, they'd rather have others be in the same boat. Like a crab trying to get out of a barrel, if undetected the others will pull you back down.

A representative from the bank finally called to inform me that they were reviewing my offer. He asked pointed questions relating to the home, repairs needed and comparable sales in the area. My initial packet to the bank's Loss Mitigation department was more than 30 pages but by the time we closed the deal it was closer to 50. Before each conversation with the mitigator I would practice in a mirror. It was important to display a strong level of confidence, in other words adopting the "act as if" principle highlighted earlier in Jackson's poem. The home was in need of repair and other houses in good condition were selling for $75,000. The owner owed $69,800 on his home. My offer to the bank minus repairs totaled $42,000. After the bank received all the paperwork needed it was time to schedule the appraisal or what is known as BPO (Brokers Price Opinion). A BPO is simply an estimate of what the properties worth in its current condition.

Four days later the appraisal came in around $40,000. This was an all cash deal so the bank gave us no more than 30 days to close. You can imagine the excitement as I negotiated thousands off my very first deal but it was far from over. Next I had to identify a buyer to purchase from me so I could pay off the bank. Most books will tell you to establish your buyer's list first, but I was so excited when I got the list that I focused on finding the deal. I then went to the papers to find ads for those looking to purchase homes. After a few calls I met my first investor. He looked over the property and decided to pay no more than $42,302 because the home was in bad shape and he had to net a high percentage on the sale once renovated. At this point, I didn't know what to do with myself. You hear about this all the time on TV, investor who makes $20,000 or $100,000 on a flip. My numbers weren't as big but I was beginning to understand the process.

We finalized the deal two weeks later and I walked away with my first check for $2,302.

I called my parents, friends and anyone else I could think of to tell. Similar to the feeling I had after the first profits from the L-block lemonade stand I was even more determined to keep going. After the first deal I would go on to flip dozens of homes making thousands of dollars, all with no money out of my pocket. It was always a win-win situation. The bank won by settling their loan, the homeowner was saved from foreclosure and I walked away making a profit simply by imagining the deal from start to finish and then following through. Once again, the sandpaper effect had become second nature and it would now be time to move on to bigger things.

Fun Parental Exercise:

Constructive Imagination *can be a tricky task for children to develop but the results are very rewarding. One of the challenges can be the abundance of toys and items available to kids today. When we were kids we didn't always get whatever we wanted so we had to be very creative when it came to having fun. One way to tap into your child's imagination involves deprivation. It sounds negative but it's a good exercise. What you need to do is deprive him/her of something and let them create a replacement. This may be tough at first but it will trigger the creative side in your child. For example: one time on the L-block it was raining very hard. We all had remote control cars and we wanted to race them in the rain. We had no concept of money and loss so we couldn't quite grasp why our parents didn't allow us to race. We were full of energy so we threw on our raincoats and headed outside. There was a small stream of water running through the middle of the back alley. There was rocks and debris in the water that would make our game more fun. We each took a piece of paper the same size and decided to have a race. You had to choose how big or small your paper would be but you had to be careful. Make it too big and it could move slowly. If it was too small it would get caught in the debris and not be able to finish the race. So we all had our sizes and we started at the top of the alley. Our parents must have thought someone got hurt when they heard the yells and screams as we cheered on these small pieces of paper in a small stream of water in a back alley. My best friend named his racer Speedy, and he lived up to his name because he beat us all, but it didn't compare to the amount of fun we had. It was so enjoyable we would soon pray for rain so we could play again. It's amazing how creative children can be when put to the test. It's like the child who gets a new toy and has more fun playing with the box than the toy. They're tapping into their imaginative side and we should encourage it as much as possible.*

10

MILLION DOLLAR TODDLER

W e've covered nine ways to spark the entrepreneurial drive in children. The key word is "spark". It's no surprise that children are full of energy and very exploratory from birth. It's our job as parents to try to steer them in the right direction and give them all the guidance and encouragement needed to succeed. This chapter is dedicated to the online site designed to help children tap into their entrepreneurial drive: www.milliondollartoddler.com. What is a Million Dollar Toddler (MDT)? To be simple, it's a child who has the drive and passion to set goals and realize their dreams despite obstacles. Sometimes we all need a push and this site will provide fun ways for children to explore the many avenues of generating income. It will force them to think and imagine what can be done in their home or neighborhood.

It's not hard to take a look in your family or neighborhood and spot that child who you know will be different. Some are able to do all sorts of things at a young age. This can be attributed to the parents providing the push or simply the child choosing to want and obtain more. The next few pages will highlight different million dollar toddlers in my life. As we get a peek of their story, visualize your child's advances and realize how important it is to stimulate this drive so they're prepared to conquer whatever may come their way.

Meet Keiasia (9 yrs old)

As a toddler, my niece Keiasia proved to be very vocal and demonstrated a strong will to succeed. As one of my two nieces she's always enjoyed having fun. Her most recent activity is Karate where she began as a white belt. Since then, she's advanced to a black stripe on white belt. She enjoys being in the 3rd grade and has been an honor roll student since the 1st grade. She was salutatorian of her kindergarten class and she's learned how to memorize things such as parts in plays and speeches.

Like most kids, Keiasia enjoys games and styling her doll baby's hair. Most notable would be her negotiation skills when it comes to gifts from her uncle. As an entrepreneur, I always try to challenge most children I meet to stimulate their creativity. While visiting one summer I gave her the option of going to Sesame Place (her favorite theme park) or receiving clothes for school. The amount for clothes would be the equivalent of spending for a day at Sesame Place (approx. $100). By giving her the <u>power of choice</u> she thought about the offer and <u>asked questions</u>. She negotiated a higher payout price for clothes and $400 later all I could do was scratch my head in wonder and hope her drive never fades.

Meet Martinique aka "Marti" (13 yrs old)

My eldest niece is certainly wise for her age. I think this is a trait she's inherited from her mom! We all watch in amazement as Marti has blossomed over the years. Although she is still very shy, we've seen her start to break out of her shell as she has journeyed through middle school.

As an eighth grader, Marti continues to maintain her perfect 4.0 academic average. She is a serious student who believes in excelling in everything. She doesn't believe in procrastinating. She realizes that being a good student is wonderful, but also aspires to be well-rounded. As a result she is part of the field hockey team, and the Business Professionals of America (BPA). These are wonderful activities for her to be a part of.

Marti has been given a real gift when it comes to writing. In elementary school she won numerous awards for her short stories and poetry, even going as far as a regional competition in the 4th grade. She is so talented and able to make characters come to life through her writing. I look forward to what her future holds because she has so much going for her.

Meet Gabriel aka "Gabe" (9 yrs old)

If I believed in reincarnation, I would definitely say that Gabe has been here before. He would have had to been an old man in that first life, because that is just what he acts like! Everyone agrees that Gabe is far beyond his nine years, especially in social settings. Just sit down and have a conversation with him. Between the extensive vocabulary he uses and the in-depth conversation topics, you would swear you were speaking with a 40-year-old!

Gabe has many endearing qualities. He is very intelligent and knowledgeable about many things. Part of that stems from his love of reading. Currently Gabe is a fourth grade student, but he is reading on an eighth grade level. When it comes to creativity, you could say that's his middle name. Whether it is creating a story, drawing, or using Manipulatives to build and create objects, Gabe always thinks outside of the box. Even with all of these qualities, one of his best character traits is his kind and sensitive heart.

He cares about everyone and always desires to see everyone treated fairly.

What does the future hold for Gabe? Of course no one has that answer, but we certainly see something dealing with technology. He is very computer savvy and if you have any problems or questions about the computer, call Gabe. It only takes once for him to see how something operates and he has it down. He says he would like to be a game designer which would fit perfectly since that's his favorite thing to do, and he certainly figures those games out very quickly. Gabe is an awesome little man!

It doesn't take a rocket scientist to read bios similar to those above and not conclude success in the future. These are just a few examples of children who are moving forward and doing great things. There were at least four different rules in each bio that the children have adopted. Success and winning are very addicting. Similar to the sparkplug for a car, the same can be applied when encouraging your child. With that said, MDT's main purpose will be to spark the entrepreneurial drive in children by teaching basic business principles through fun, interactive games. The target age range will be 4-10.

They say self-esteem is critical to proper child development. Just think of your own self-confidence and how that has helped you progress to your current plot in life. Practice makes perfect, and the more we do something the more proficient we become. Kids will face many challenges as they get older, therefore, self-esteem can act as the armor needed to protect them. A child with good self-esteem will have an easier time handling conflicts and negative pressures than one without.

A by-product of MDT will be propelling a child's self-esteem. Self-esteem is a realistic respect for or favorable impression of oneself, our self-perceptions. These patterns of good or bad self-esteem start at a very young age, hence the program's focus on targeting toddlers. It's quite amazing how quickly a child develops the drive to want to be successful. Just think of the traditional high-five. Most kids learn the high-five fairly early. It's a way to smack hands in a congratulatory way, even though they may not know what the occasion may be. The son of a good friend is very active and into sports. Whenever I see him we have the high-five duel or challenge. It excites me to see how passionate he gets after each high five. He has this look on his face that says "indestructible" and the more I cheer him on, the harder and more efficient he becomes.

The games on MDT are a compilation of things we used to do as kids to create income. From the lemonade stand to selling Avon for a day, we were relentless in our pursuits. We realized it was best to explore and fail numerous times as kids because we had the safety net of our parents to fall back on.

The more money we made the more the hunger grew. To date, we've all been very successful whether we work for others or ourselves. Had we not explored the many facets of being an entrepreneur while kids, the fear would take over and the spark would never mature into the flame. As I wrote the last chapter of this book it became clear what rule #10 would be – ***Constant Learning!*** Since the drive began as a toddler we never once hit our peak so the question could be whether one exists or not. In the introduction a question was asked: Can we have whatever we want or desire? It becomes an understatement when we view the countless examples of those who have accomplished many insurmountable feats. Similar to rule #2 (exposure), constant learning is addicting once nurtured. There are millions of books available in our hometown libraries and bookstores. Topics range from business to cooking recipes or how-to's on any theme you can imagine. It's been said that knowledge is power. Some also say luck is when preparation meets opportunity. Both statements materialize into reality when we reach out and grab what we feel is owed to us.

Fun Parental Exercise:

When parents make things fun and exciting, kids look forward to these activities. To some Constant Learning can be challenging. Electronics and entertainment are in abundance these days, so children are naturally drawn by the glitz and glamour they provide. Enrolling in a good reading program can make things enjoyable. You can set one up yourself by offering prizes or rewards for them completing certain books. This ties in with rule #2 (exposure) and will help your child explore all types of paths as they mature. You could take it a step further make it a weekly prize when they complete a certain amount of hours on their book. A simple trip to the library can help make the journey more appealing. Seeing your child choose his/her own book is like watching them set a goal and plan to accomplish it.

Some remember their childhood as being a time of fun and excitement, while others experienced the opposite. No matter the intellectual level, one cannot deny the importance of education when it comes to children. No other being has the capacity to learn so much in a short period of time. Many of us grow up to remain kids, but we can never go back to the stage of walking for the first time or learning to speak. Million Dollar Toddler's supreme goal is to spark the entrepreneurial drive in children. Below is a poem I found online. The author's unknown and some may have read it before, but the message is clear:

One hundred years from now,
It will not matter,
What kind of car I drove,
What kind of house I lived in,

How much I had in my bank,

Nor what my clothes looked like.

One hundred years from now,

It will not matter,

What kind of school I attended,

What kind of typewriter I used,

How large or small my church.

But the world may be. . .

A little better because. . .

I was important in the life of a child.

Take a close look at your child. If you have no children, envision your niece/nephew or simply a child on whom you've had some sort of impact. Fast forward to each phase of their life and see the awards coming, the different lives they're influencing along with the drive to duplicate the process by teaching others. They will depict what the future will be. With that said, it's critical that we continue to supply what's needed to keep them craving for more.

In some parts of the country children are a means of cheap labor. Just think what this can do to a child's self-esteem. If we don't continue to nurture and show our kids how truly important they are, we could be setting them up for failure. I applaud you for taking the first step in learning the 10 ways to spark the entrepreneur in your child. What's the next step? Continue to apply the rules by challenging them in loving ways. These principles and guidelines will remain with them forever.